Contents

Some words are shown in bold, **like this**.
You can find them in the glossary on page 23.

What is a badger?

A badger is a small **mammal**. It has a short tail, strong legs and a long snout.

A badger has long claws to help it dig deep holes.

You might wonder why you don't see badgers outside during the day.

This is because they are **nocturnal**.

What does nocturnal mean?

Nocturnal animals are awake at night.

Animals that are nocturnal sleep during the day.

Many different animals are nocturnal.

Bats, owls, foxes and mice are nocturnal.

Where do badgers live?

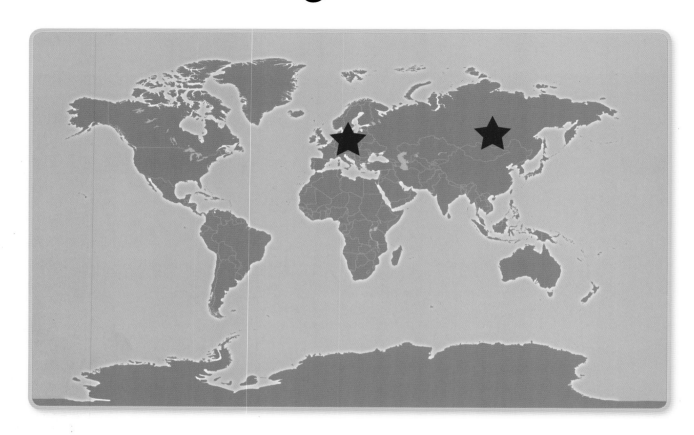

Badgers live in many parts of the world.

This book shows the European badger. This type of badger lives in Europe and Asia.

Most badgers live in wooded areas.

Badgers can also be found in parks, grasslands and even on some farmland.

What do badgers eat?

Badgers are good hunters.

They eat small mammals, such as mice.

Badgers also eat plants, such as berries and grains.

Do badgers have predators?

Most badgers are the largest **predators** in their area.

This means they hunt other animals for food.

Badgers have few predators.

Pet dogs sometimes hunt badgers for food.

What are badger babies like?

Female badgers give birth to one **litter** each year.

A litter usually has between two and five baby badgers.

Baby badgers are covered in soft, light grey fur.

Their eyes stay closed until they are four to five weeks old.

What is a badger sett?

Badgers dig special tunnels called **setts**.

Badger setts can be very long with many openings.

Many badgers can live in a single sett.

Badgers keep their setts very clean.

How can you spot badgers?

The best time to spot a badger is at **dusk** or **dawn**.

Large holes dug into the ground could be entrances to badger setts.

Badgers often dig their setts into hillsides or at the bottoms of trees.

Badgers live in groups. If you see one, keep your eyes peeled for others!

How should you treat badgers?

If you spot a badger, try to stay very quiet.

Watch the badger from a safe distance.

Never try to touch a badger. Some badgers carry diseases that can harm humans.

If badgers get scared, they may bite and scratch.

Badger body map

leg

tail

snout

claw

Picture glossary

 **dawn** time of day when the sun first rises

 **dusk** time of day when the sun sets

 **litter** group of baby animals born from the same mother at the same time

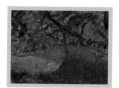 **mammal** warm-blooded animal that has a backbone, hair or fur, and gives birth to live babies that feed on milk from their mother

 **nocturnal** awake at night and asleep during the day

 **predator** animal that hunts other animals for food

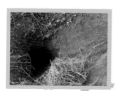 **setts** long tunnels badgers dig under the ground

23

Find out more

Books

British Mammals (Nature Detective), Victoria Munson (Wayland, 2014)

Badger (British Animals), Michael Leach (Wayland, 2010)

Websites

Discover more nocturnal animals at:
www.bbc.co.uk/nature/adaptations/Nocturnality

Learn more about badgers at:
www.rspca.org.uk/allaboutanimals/wildlife/inthewild/badgers

Index

Raintree is an imprint of Capstone Global Library Limited, a company incorporated in England and Wales having its registered office at 7 Pilgrim Street, London, EC4V 6LB – Registered company number: 6695582

www.raintreepublishers.co.uk
myorders@raintreepublishers.co.uk

Text © Capstone Global Library Limited 2015
First published in hardback in 2014
First published in paperback in 2015
The moral rights of the proprietor have been asserted.

Edited by Brynn Baker, Clare Lewis, and
      Helen Cox Cannons
Designed by Kyle Grenz and Tim Bond
Picture research by Tracy Cummins
Production by Helen McCreath
Originated by Capstone Global Library Limited
Printed and bound in China by Leo Paper Group

ISBN 978-1-406-28285-6 (hardback)
18 17 16 15 14
10 9 8 7 6 5 4 3 2 1

ISBN 978-1-406-28292-4 (paperback)
19 18 17 16 15
10 9 8 7 6 5 4 3 2 1

British Library Cataloguing in Publication Data
A full catalogue record for this book is available from the British Library.

Acknowledgements
We would like to thank the following for permission to reproduce photographs: Alamy: © FLPA, 6; FLPA: Derek Middleton, 17, 7 mouse, Hugo Willcox/FN/Minden, 10, Imagebroker, 7 owl, John Eveson, 18, 23a, Martin B Withers, 14, 15, 19, 23b, 23c, Michael Durham/Minden Pictures, 7 bat, Paul Hobson, 11, Richard Costin, 5, 21, 23e, Robert Canis, 22, Sean Hunter, 16, 23g; Getty Images: Nature Picture Library/Britain On View, front cover; Shutterstock: Andrew Astbury, 7 fox, Devin Koob, 13, 23f, KOO, 4, 20, 23d, back cover, MARKABOND, 12, OlegDoroshin, 9

Every effort has been made to contact copyright holders of material reproduced in this book. Any omissions will be rectified in subsequent printings if notice is given to the publisher.

All the internet addresses (URLs) given in this book were valid at the time of going to press. However, due to the dynamic nature of the internet, some addresses may have changed, or sites may have changed or ceased to exist since publication. While the author and publisher regret any inconvenience this may cause readers, no responsibility for any such changes can be accepted by either the author or the publisher.

Rebecca Rissman

raintree